SUMMIT UP

Riddles about Mountains

by June Swanson
pictures by Susan Slattery Burke

Lerner Publications Company · Minneapolis

To Sandy and Steve, who both love the mountains —J.S.
To my wonderful daughter, Perrin, for her inspiration in this first year
 of her life —S.S.B.

Copyright © 1994 by Lerner Publications Company

This book is available in two editions:
Library binding by Lerner Publications Company
Soft cover by First Avenue Editions
241 First Avenue North
Minneapolis, MN 55401

Library of Congress Cataloging-in-Publication Data

Swanson, June.
  Summit up : riddles about mountains / by June Swanson ; pictures
by Susan Slattery Burke.
    p.   cm. — (You must be joking!)
  Summary: A collection of riddles about mountains, including
"What did the Swiss hiker yell as he fell down the mountain?
Alp! Alp!"
  ISBN 0-8225-2342-6 (lib. bdg.)
  1. Riddles, Juvenile. 2. Mountains—Juvenile humor. [1. Mountains—
Wit and humor. 2. Riddles. 3. Jokes.] I. Burke, Susan Slattery, ill.
II. Title. III. Series.
PN6371.5.S87 1994
818'.5402—dc20   93-19157
                                                          CIP
                                                          AC
Manufactured in the United States of America

1 2 3 4 5 6 – I/JR – 99 98 97 96 95 94

Q: What's the wettest mountain in the world?

A: Mount Rainier.

Q: What kind of ears do the Smoky Mountains have?
A: Mountaineers.

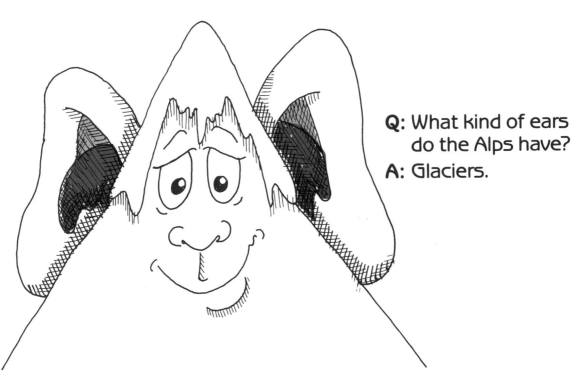

Q: What kind of ears do the Alps have?
A: Glaciers.

Q: Why did the robber steal Mount Rushmore?

A: He took it for granite.

Q: What did the sheriff say after he climbed the mountain?

A: "I need arrest."

Q: Do you think those mountain goats know where Mount McKinley is?

A: I don't know. Alaska goat and find out.

Q: Why did the kitten meow all day?

A: She was practicing her Cat-skills.

Q: Why couldn't the mountain keep a secret?

A: Its brooks babbled everything.

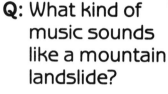

Q: What kind of
music sounds
like a mountain
landslide?

A: Rock and roll.

Q: What do you have when 400
wild blueberries try to get
down the mountain at the
same time?

A: A blueberry jam.

Q: Why did everyone laugh at the mountain?
A: Because it was hill-arious.

Q: What's the difference between a hill and a pill?
A: A hill is hard to get up, and a pill is hard to get down.

Q: When is a mountain like a car out of gas?
A: When it's MT.

Q: What do you find in both a hill and a mountain?
A: The letter "i."

Q: What instrument did the little Alp want to play?
A: A Matter-horn.

Q: What did O call her boat?
A: Ozark.

Q: What did the bear use when he played baseball on the mountain?

A: His sum-mitt.

Q: What would you have if Mount Rushmore threw a football to Pike's Peak?

A: A mountain pass.

Q: What did one mountain say to the other mountain after the earthquake?

A: "Don't look at me. It wasn't my fault!"

Q: What did the baby eagle say to her sisters as they pecked open their shells?

A: "Last one out is a rotten egg!"

Q: What did the three bears use to close their house on the mountain?

A: Goldi-locks.

Q: Why did the ballerina go to a flat place on the mountain?

A: To do a pla-teau dance.

Q: Why wouldn't the skeleton climb the mountain?

A: He didn't have the guts to do it.

Q: How could you tell the artist was tired of drawing mountains?

A: He went back to the drawing bored.

Q: How did the Big Bad Wolf know the Little Pig was building a strong house in the mountains?

A: He saw Himalayan the bricks.

Q: Did you hear that the Abominable Snowman moved into the ski lodge?

A: Now that's an ugly roomer!

Q: What do you get if you cross Pike's Peak with an alarm clock?

A: Mountain time.

Q: What do you get if you cross Pike's Peak with a pair of sandals?

A: Cold feet.

Q: What has 14,162 feet and no legs?

A: Mount Shasta.

Q: What lives in the Rockies and is red and black and white all over?

A: A ladybug in a snowstorm.

Q: When is a mountain goat most likely to go into a log cabin?

A: When the door is open.

Q: What has four wheels, two horns, and goes from rock to rock up the mountainside?

A: A bighorn sheep on a skateboard.

Q: Who crosses the mountain going trip-trap-giggle, trip-trap-giggle, trip-trap-giggle?
A: The three silly goats gruff.

Q: What did Dorothy say as she climbed the mountain?
A: "Lions and goats and bears, oh my!"

Q: How does Peter Pan find his cow in the Alps?
A: He listens for her Tinkerbell.

Q: Why did the mountain goats and the bighorn sheep meet on the mountaintop?
A: They knew two herds are better than one.

Q: What did the skier say when she fell through the ice?
A: "You can't judge a brook by its cover."

Q: In what month was the little Alp born?
A: Alp-ril.

Q: What did the little Alp eat at noon?
A: Her avalunch.

Q: Why was the father hill worried about the baby hill?
A: He was afraid the baby would never a-mountain much.

Q: How did the Himalayan explorer get up the mountain?

A: By yak back.

Q: How did he carry his food?

A: In his yak backpack.

Q: What lives in the Himalayas and is black and white and red all over?

A: A sunburned panda.

Q: Why did the bare
mountaintop blush?

A: He thought the other
mountains were
peaking at him.

Q: Why did the bear
look for a scale
on the mountain?

A: Because where
there's a hill,
there's a weigh.

Q: Where did the fisherman cook his Rocky Mountain trout?

A: On the mountain range.

Q: What happened after the camper waited for the sun to rise over the mountain?

A: It finally dawned on him.

Q: What falls on the mountain and never gets hurt?

A: Snow.

Q: Where is Smokey Bear's hat?

A: On top of old Smokey.

Q: What did one volcano say to the other volcano?

A: ''Do you lava me?''

Q: Why was the mountain climber sad?
A: She was wearing her blue jeans.

Q: What did the astronaut start when she climbed the mountain?
A: An avalaunch.

Q: What did the Swiss hiker yell as he fell down the mountain?
A: ''Alp! Alp!''

Q: What did the cowpoke say when he tried to saddle the moving horse?

A: "Doesn't this Mount Everest?"

Q: What's the weather like on Mount Everest?

A: I don't know. I've never been able to climate.

Q: What did the beaver say to the aspen?

A: "It's been nice gnawing you."

Q: Why was the little mountain pine always warm?

A: Because he was a fir tree.

Q: Why was the sun waiting for spring to come to the mountain?

A: It wanted to burn over a new leaf.

Q: Why did the hunter shoot the aspen in winter?

A: He wanted to put a cartridge in a bare tree.

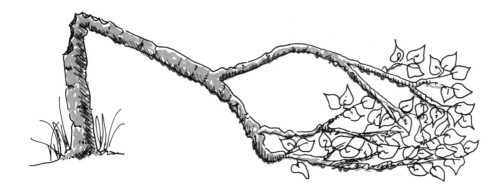

Q: How did the little fir tree eat his ice cream?
A: In a pinecone.

Q: What was the little fir tree's favorite drink?
A: Mountain dew.

Q: Why did the little cloud want to leave the mountain and go to school?
A: He liked to snow and tell.

Q: Why was everyone running around the mountain looking for a female deer?
A: Because every time they passed doe, they collected $200.

Q: Why did the bear cross the road?

A: Because there weren't any chickens on the mountain.

Q: Why wouldn't the old bear climb the mountain?

A: She was already over the hill.

Q: Who is green and never comes down off the mountain?

A: Hermit the Frog.

Q: Where did the bighorn sheep get his hair cut?

A: In a baa-baa shop.

Q: What did the mother mountain goat say when she found her baby asleep?

A: "There'll be no kid-napping around here!"

Q: What do you call a dog who lives on a mountaintop?

A: A chilly dog.

Q: What would you call a yellow stripe painted down a mountainside?

A: A mountain lion.

Q: What did the glacier's bumper sticker say?

A: "Have an ice day!"

ABOUT THE AUTHOR

June Swanson began her career by writing magazine articles and short stories. After having almost 200 published—for both children and adults—she turned to writing books. This is her fifth published book. June is a graduate of the University of Texas, and she has a master's degree in English from Florida Atlantic University. She lives in New Hampshire and enjoys hiking, skiing, collecting antiques, and visiting her four children and nine grandchildren.

ABOUT THE ARTIST

Susan Slattery Burke loves to illustrate fun-loving characters, especially animals. To her, each of her characters has a personality all its own. She is most satisfied when the characters come to life for the reader as well. Susan lives in Minnetonka, Minnesota, with her husband, two daughters, and their dog and cat. Susan enjoys sculpting, reading, traveling, illustrating, and chasing her children around.

You Must Be Joking books

Alphabatty
Riddles from A to Z

Help Wanted
Riddles about Jobs

Here's to Ewe
Riddles about Sheep

Hide and Shriek
Riddles about Ghosts and Goblins

Ho Ho Ho!
Riddles about Santa Claus

Home on the Range
Ranch-Style Riddles

Hoop-La
Riddles about Basketball

I Toad You So
Riddles about Frogs and Toads

Off Base
Riddles about Baseball

On with the Show
Show Me Riddles

Out on a Limb
Riddles about Trees and Plants

Out to Dry
Riddles about Deserts

Summit Up
Riddles about Mountains

Take a Hike
Riddles about Football

That's for Shore
Riddles from the Beach

Weather or Not
Riddles for Rain and Shine

What's Gnu?
Riddles from the Zoo

Wing It!
Riddles about Birds